For Ana
and Francisco

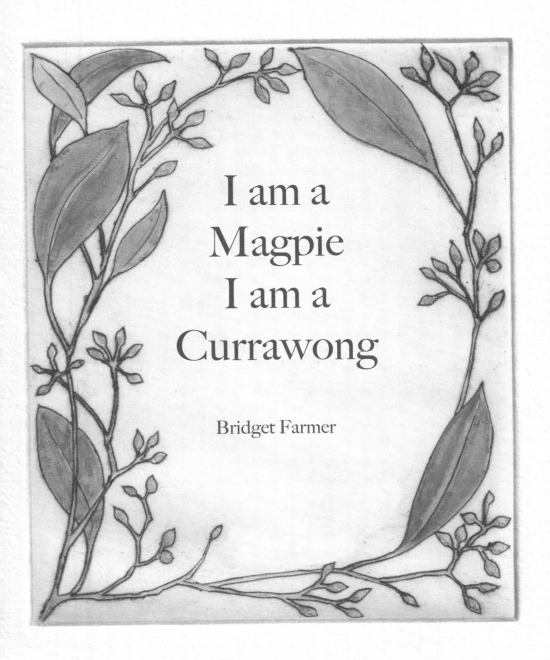

# I am a
# Magpie
# I am a
# Currawong

Bridget Farmer

I am a
magpie,
not one to
be shy.

I am a
currawong,
with a
yellow eye.

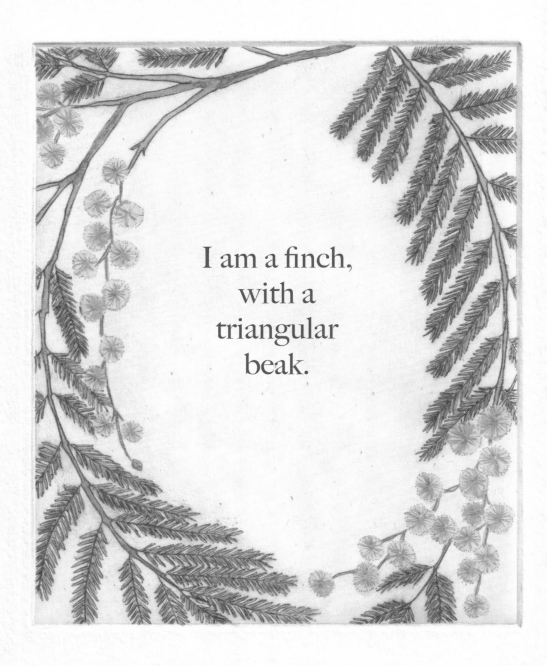

I am a finch,
with a
triangular
beak.

I am a duck,
swimming
in the creek.

I am a
thornbill,
high up in
the tree.

I am a tern,
living by
the sea.

I am a
kestrel,
hovering
over the
field.

I am a
quail,
quiet and
concealed.

I am a
heron,
standing
very still.

I am a
honeyeater,
drinking
my fill.

I am a rosella,
a colourful
delight.

I am an owl,
awake by
night.

# Featured
# Birds

Australian Magpie
Pied Currawong
Finches (top to bottom)
Red-browed Finch
Zebra Finch
Double-barred Finch
Australian Wood Duck
Striated Thornbills
Little Tern
Nankeen / Australian Kestrel
Stubble Quail
White-faced Heron
Honeyeaters
(left) New Holland Honeyeater
(right) Eastern Spinebill
Eastern Rosella
Southern Boobook

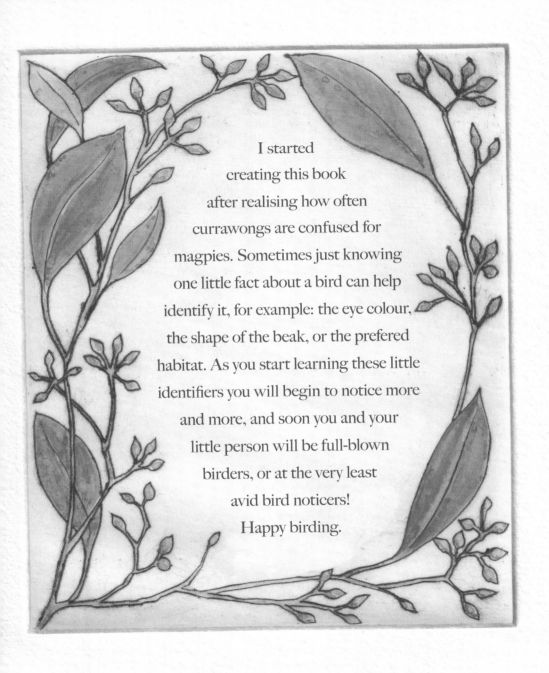

I started
creating this book
after realising how often
currawongs are confused for
magpies. Sometimes just knowing
one little fact about a bird can help
identify it, for example: the eye colour,
the shape of the beak, or the prefered
habitat. As you start learning these little
identifiers you will begin to notice more
and more, and soon you and your
little person will be full-blown
birders, or at the very least
avid bird noticers!
Happy birding.

Published
in Australia by Black
Cockatoo Books
www.blackcockatoobooks.com.au

Text and illustration copyright
© Bridget Farmer 2024

Email: bridget@bridgetfarmerprintmaker.com
www.bridgetfarmerprintmaker.com

I would like to acknowledge the Aboriginal and
Torres Strait Islander people who are the traditional
custodians of the land that has inspired this book.

ISBN 978-0-6457137-2-5

The text for this book is set in Big Caslon.
The illustrations for this book are
drypoint etchings hand coloured in
watercolour paint.

Original illustrations, words, cover and
internal design by Bridget Farmer.
Pre-press by Subgreen
Printed in China by
China Printing Masters.